BARBARA PEARCE

ARRANGING FLOWERS

HAMLYN

Produced by New Leaf Productions

Photography by Mick Duff
Design by Jim Wire
Typeset by System Graphics
Series Editor: Elizabeth Gibson

First published in 1985 by
The Hamlyn Publishing Group Limited
Bridge House, 69 London Road
Twickenham, Middlesex, England

Second impression 1987

ISBN 0 600 30647 X

Printed in Hong Kong by Mandarin Offset

CONTENTS

We would like to thank:
Hillier's Garden Centre, London Road, Windlesham,
Surrey; also Notcutts Garden Centre, Waterers Nurseries,
Bagshot, Surrey; and Elliots Floral (Camberley) Limited,
3 & 5 Grace Reynolds Walk, Camberley, Surrey.

INTRODUCTION

This book gives guidelines for creating flower arrangements in the home—guidelines that make the arrangements easier to achieve. The book will also aid those who arrange flowers in churches, offices and hospitals. Once you have mastered the basic shapes of the arrangements, you can easily develop your own personal style by following the suggestions given.

Separate sections of the book describe where the plant material can be obtained, what to look for when buying from a florist and what to select from a garden and countryside. Whether you buy flowers or cut them from the garden, you can adapt the various styles of arrangements in the book to endless combinations of plant material, especially since for each arrangement I have suggested alternative flowers and foliage, where possible keeping the flowers to their seasons.

The book explains in detail how to look after the flowers and foliage—both before and after arranging them—how to choose suitable plant material for the container, how to place them to best advantage, and how to choose the right container. (Most flower arrangers refer to vases as containers, probably because bowls and dishes often used for flowers are not specifically made for arrangements but designed for other purposes.)

General Hints

An arrangement needs to be as natural as possible, so take into consideration the shape and curve of the stem and how flowers and foliage grow. A particularly upright plant is best placed upright in the arrangement. Curved stems look better over the rim of the container than straight ones coming out at unnatural angles. Face some flowers sideways—not directly facing the front of the arrangement.

All the stems of both flowers and foliage should appear to be growing from a central point, a point determined by the tallest vertical flower or foliage in the arrangement. Have all the stems radiating from this point though only a few will actually reach it (as on this page).

Place something special at the centre (or focal point) of the arrangement; the eye looks at the centre and then travels to the rest of the arrangement. Use an uneven number of large flowers, or use special flowers, or use a deeper colour at the centre. An uneven number of large leaves or a rosette of leaves in the centre gives the impression of holding the arrangement together.

When the flowers and leaves come well out over the edge of the vase, the flowers and vase merge to form a unified arrangement—but check the stems are all obtaining water.

Uneven numbers of flowers are easier to arrange; if an even number is used, it is easy to place the flowers in pairs and get too formal a pattern, especially with multiples of four which form a square. Uneven numbers however, allow you to zigzag them through. This only applies when fewer than twelve flowers are used.

Avoid stems that cross each other and make removal difficult when one has been incorrectly placed.

Balance the arrangement well so the "weight" of the plant material looks approximately the same on each side. Use smaller materials towards the edges and higher throughout it, and larger nearer the centre and lower in the container.

It is always better to do an arrangement where it is to be placed. When this is not practical, however, it is helpful to arrange flowers at the height at which they will be situated. Their effect can be spoiled if the arrangement is moved to a higher or lower level.

Try to have plant material at various levels throughout the arrangement. Some need to be recessed, some long, and some in medium lengths to make the arrangement more irregular; a flower should not be the same length as the one beside it. The peripheral flowers should project in and out alternately, giving the design an unevenness.

Do not place so many flowers in the container that they are wasted. Remember buds open into larger flowers; leave extra space around them to avoid overcrowding. The mechanics such as wire netting and florists' foam need to be covered with small pieces of foliage and short flowers.

At times you need only use foliage. These arrangements can look particularly cool in the summer. The use of berries and rich coloured foliage is most attractive in the autumn. In winter fresh plant material need not be used at all, as flowers can be very costly; instead dried plant material or silk flowers can be substituted—silk flowers are becoming increasingly popular. When using either preserved or silk flowers, however, it is important not to leave an arrangement too long before mixing its flowers with some other varieties or colours in different containers.

Any arrangement can be made either larger or smaller as required, since the proportions of an arrangement are the same whether it is miniature or a pedestal group. The size of the flower would naturally need to vary accordingly.

CONTAINERS

The introduction mentions that any receptacle used for flower arrangements is known as a container. Some are easier to arrange than others: the container with the large opening is generally simpler than one with a small opening. For this reason it is advisable to begin with one that has a large diameter such as a bowl or tazza.

Part of the enjoyment of flower arranging is to choose a container suitable for the flowers. The colour, the type of flower and the shape of the arrangement to be created all need to be taken into consideration. The colour of the flowers should blend well with the container to create a unified final arrangement, the flowers sometimes being the same colour as the container, sometimes contrasting. Usually a coloured china or pottery container looks better with an arrangement of flowers of the same colour, or at least a selection which includes its own colour. Green containers are most versatile and will quite happily take different coloured flower arrangements as well as a variety of green plant material. White vases look pleasant with white and pastel shades rather than with reds and oranges as these contrast too sharply. Neutrally coloured china and pottery are also useful since they may be used with many different plant materials and colours. Metal containers such as brass, copper, silver, pewter and wrought iron can look dramatic with flowers in them. Silver, for instance, looks pretty with white and pink and especially at Christmas with red, though it does not lend itself particularly well to oranges and yellows. Brass is ideal for yellow plant material and also for orange and green. Copper is superb with warm colours. Pewter can be delightful with pink, blue and mauve, either individually or in combination. Wrought iron takes many flower colours as it is usually black. Variously shaped baskets are useful in arranging orange, red and yellow flowers, and they readily accept a mixture of all flower colours. Glass is exceptionally pleasing with white or paler shades, and green looks particularly cool in it during the summer. Many other colour compositions are possible; these are just a few suggestions. Later you will want to experiment with a wide variety of flowers and containers, discovering unusual colour schemes that make quite startling arrangements.

The type of flowers you choose can make or spoil a certain container. An exotic orchid like the cattleya would look uncomfortable in a basket; whereas it would look beautiful in porcelain or silver. On the other hand some of the less exotic orchids such as the spider orchid are attractive in bamboo containers. Hothouse-grown roses looking more fragile than robust garden ones are better placed in a more delicate container; whereas the garden ones look quite at home in a basket. Most flowers of the garden type are good in basketwork, unless the flowers are particularly delicate such as outdoor-grown freesia. Dried and preserved materials (especially those grown in the garden) are suited more to wood, brass, heavy pottery and basketwork containers but fragile-looking dried flowers can successfully be arranged in a variety of other containers.

The shape, colour and texture of the arrangement should determine which container is used. The all-round arrangement looks ill at ease in a narrow-necked vase; without sufficient space at the top to give the correct proportions, the arrangement can look as if it is perched on the top rather than a complete unit. All-rounds are better in tazzas, bowls, round baskets—with or without a handle—or similar circular containers. Facing arrangements can be created in such containers as tazzas, urns, cylinders, shells, baskets, bowls and troughs, with due consideration given to the height and width of the container—whether it is low and spreading, tall and slender or in basic proportions. Asymmetrical facing arrangements look at ease in similarly shaped containers. A vase which is very narrow at the top can be "widened" by the placement of a candlecup at the top to give a larger area for the arrangement. The urn and cylinder will take fewer flowers than the tazza or bowl; the cylinder in particular looks exceptionally good with a simple arrangement of a few twigs and three or five flowers. An oblong or oval container looks attractive with a table centre arrangement at the centre of a similarly shaped table; a round table should have a low, all-round arrangement. The container for a table centre should in fact always be fairly low. Any container stem should not be too high as the height would block the view across the table. For an L-shaped arrangement a trough or oval container is ideal; a lidded basket holds an L-

shape very satisfactorily, too. Simple line arrangements similar to Japanese flower arrangements (although these are a different art form) look lovely on plates or flat dishes when a small container is placed on them with either a piece of florists' foam or a pinholder in it. Troughs can also be used for them. When you use dried or silk flowers in such arrangements, you will need dry florists' foam.

When purchasing flower containers to begin arranging, choose a vase which could be used for more than one type of arrangement. A tazza, for example, would be suitable for a facing arrangement (symmetrical or asymmetrical) and for an all-round; a trough could be used for a table centre, an L-shaped, line, and for facing arrangements—but not for an all-round.

As well as buying vases manufactured for the purpose, you can find innumerable containers around the house. A large pedestal group suitable for a church or reception can be placed in a large pastry bowl. Pottery pastry bowls bought especially for arrangements could be painted with matt finish paint in a colour suitable to the flowers. (Matt paint is preferable as it is less noticeable than gloss.) The stand of a fondue set is an attractive container for a line arrangement, as is a meat dish, especially a plain one

(although a patterned one could be used to pick up the colours from the flowers.) Most jugs and tankards are ideal, arranged asymmetrically, particularly pewter tankards with pink flowers in them.

Take care not to spoil the containers after the arrangement has died and the flowers are thrown away; make sure you clean out the container well before putting more flowers in it; this helps prevent the surface from becoming stained. If the copper, brass, pewter or silver containers are valuable, take care not to scratch them with the wire netting or wire. Sticky tape used to hold the netting can mark the surface; instead, use florists' foam. Alabaster vases should have a lining in them; often a polythene container that fits can be found. If this is not possible, use the container for dried or silk flowers.

EQUIPMENT

The most important equipment in flower arranging is the aid which holds the flowers securely into the container: wire netting, florists' foam, or a pinholder. *Wire netting* is the least expensive and will last indefinitely. It is preferable to use the 50-mm/2-inch mesh; a slightly smaller mesh can be used, but it may cause problems if the holes are not large enough to enable you to insert thicker stems (for example daffodils) without splitting them. 50-mm/2-inch mesh allows room for the thick stems and can be pushed closer together for the thinner ones. The amount of netting needed varies with the thickness of the stems and the size of the container. Generally the stems of spring flowers are thicker than those of the rest of the year, so less netting is required at this time. When putting the netting into the container, use one piece; if only two smaller pieces are available, twist the edges of these together to form one piece. Roll the netting fairly loosely diagonally across from one corner to the opposite one—making three, four or five layers, depending on the size of the container. Then shape the netting to the vase; if the vase is round, both sides of the netting are bent to form a ball; if rectangular, they are bent in a little way to form the correct shape; if an urn is used, bend one end over, then place the other end into the container first. Make sure some of the netting touches the base of the vase. Sometimes a pinholder or florists' foam is used underneath the netting to hold heavier stems. Distribute the netting evenly throughout the container, raising it towards the centre. Clip several pieces of the netting over the edge if the vase has a lip; if not tie it as for a parcel with reel wire or thin string.

Florists' foam is a water-retaining substance that can be bought from florists and garden centres in bricks and small rounds. One of the makes is called Oasis. Before you use the florists' foam it needs to thoroughly soak under water, weighted to keep it down, and left—preferably overnight but at least two hours. If the water is not allowed to reach the centre of the block, the flowers could go into a dry patch and consequently die. You can cut florists' foam to the required shape and size whether it is wet or dry. Cutting it when dry is probably less wasteful so that you do not soak more than you require for a vase. If you are using florists' foam on its own in a container, it goes slightly above the rim, with space around the edge to enable you to fill it up with water easily, since the foam dries out quickly in a warm room.

Florists' foam can also be used under wire netting. When creating some line arrangements, place a piece of it in a small container on the plate and then place the flowers in the foam. If the flowers are heavy, it is advisable to have a piece of wire netting over the foam; alternatively, place the foam onto a heavy pinholder to stabilise the heavy stems. A special pinholder with fewer spikes is obtainable for this purpose. Florists' foam is especially good for small arrangements such as in a goblet; a gift arrangement can be transported without the water spilling. The foam can be used two or three times before it disintegrates.

Pinholders come in various sizes and shapes: round, crescent and oblong. They are mainly for line arrangements, usually on a fairly shallow dish or plate. If the container is too shallow to hold enough water to cover it, place it in a small receptacle. Otherwise the water is poured into the container as usual and looks attractive beneath the flowers. Sometimes line arrangements are on wooden or basketwork trays; in this case a small dish is essential and it needs to be topped up with water regularly, especially initially as the flowers will take up much water. Pinholders under netting are most helpful to hold heavier stems. Place them three-quarters of the way back in the vase for a facing arrangement, in the centre for an all-round or table centre, and to one side for the L-shaped arrangement.

Flower-cutting scissors are available for flower arranging and are obtainable from florists and garden centres. These cut not only heavy flower stems but also wire netting, some having a groove at the base of the blade for this reason. Really heavy stems may need to be cut with secateurs.

Silver reel wire is bought on reels and is similar to fuse wire. Use it for tying wire netting into some containers. It can also be bought in black but will rust if in contact with water. If the reel wire is difficult to obtain, you can substitute thin string. When netting is tied in with the reel wire, the reel wire should be removed once the flowers are arranged if it is visible. Once properly balanced the flowers should be stable enough to stay in position in the netting.

Stub wires are straight wires in various gauges which are used mainly when fruit, vegetables, fir cones, dried flower heads and such like are used in an arrangement. They provide false stems for them so that these materials are more securely positioned in the wire netting.

Cones or tubes are a help when more height is required to obtain the correct proportions in an arrangement, or when the flower stems are not sufficiently long—especially when you create a pedestal group. To make the cones taller use a square stick, preferably painted green to disguise it amongst foliage, and attach it to the lower half of the cone with sticky tape. They are also useful in a planted garden on a dish if you require a few flowers to brighten the garden when the pot plants are not flowering. Place cones firmly into the soil; fill with water and arrange the flowers in them. When using the cones both in a container or for a planted garden, you can place a small piece of florists' foam or wire netting into them to hold the flowers firmly.

Candlecups are used in flower arrangements when you are creating an arrangement on a candlestick or candelabrum. They are small round bowls of metal or plastic which have a stem to fit the top of the candlestick. Wire netting or florists' foam is put into the candlecup, the candle placed through the centre into the recess of the candlecup, and flowers and leaves then arranged round it. The most suitable shape is an all-round one, arranged somewhat lower than other all-rounds. When using a three-branched candelabrum, it is better to have either a candlecup at each end or one in the centre; all three are rather overpowering. The candlecup is helpful placed on top of a narrow-necked container, or in bottle arrangements for informal parties.

Candle holders are small metal or plastic holders with spikes at the base. When you are using a candle in an arrangement you can place the candle in the holder and the holder in the netting, pinholder or florists' foam to stabilise it.

A long-spouted watering can is convenient for watering of the arrangements; a *spray-mister* is also useful for overhead watering. To save much tidying up after arranging the flowers, a *dust sheet* is always handy, even at home.

An added bonus are a range of various *coloured pebbles or shells*. Have about five or seven of each colour, in different sizes, and place them on the dish in a line arrangement to help to cover the pinholder and to show beneath the flowers. *Driftwood* or interesting shapes of wood, pieces of tree roots or bare heather plants are extra materials useful as accessories to simple flower arrangements, again mainly on flat dishes and plates, reducing the number of flowers required.

FLOWERS AND FOLIAGE

OBTAINING PLANT MATERIAL

The availability of plant material is governed to a certain extent by where you live. Usual sources of flowers and foliage are gardens, balconies, flower shops, garden centres, nurserymen, street traders, and the countryside.

If you have a garden, you can grow many plants especially for arranging. If space is limited, you can concentrate on foliage rather than flowers; foliage arrangements do please the eye, and you can always buy flowers. You can also grow plants to preserve for winter when other plant material is scarce.

A balcony or window box is well worth planting with a few foliage plants, and if you have cooking herbs, use them to go with the flowers purchased at the florist for your flower arrangements.

If you are buying from the florist you will have a wide range of flowers to choose from, though the choice of foliage is often small. Foliage from pot plants bought from a florist or garden centre is a great help; cut it and it will grow more leaves. All foliage is precious when you have to rely on the florist for it, so any leaves and stems removed from a flower should be retained. If possible keep a piece of stem with the leaf; cut away the top part of the stem to where the leaf is growing, leaving the stem below the leaf to assist in securing the foliage in the container. Rose leaves are useful when placed in this way. Tulip leaves can be rather long and untidy, so cut the leaf to a reasonable length. Roll a separate piece of stem (taken from the flower stem) at the bottom of the leaf, again to hold the leaf more firmly in the arrangement. Sometimes the leaves of carnations (or "grasses" as they are known) are helpful as a foliage when bought in bunches or actually taken from the flower stems.

Preserved material and silk flowers can be purchased from flower shops, departmental stores and garden centres, which usually offer a wide range of both flowers and foliage. You can also obtain fruit, vegetables, fir cones for use in arrangements with flowers and foliage—to assist in colour schemes and to reduce the number of flowers required.

Nurserymen will often sell direct to you. Generally they do not offer a large choice of flowers as they tend to specialise in one or two varieties, but because the flowers do not have to travel to a market before reaching the shop they are very fresh. Chrysanthemums, carnations, roses and others can be purchased in this way. Some nurseries will pack boxes of special foliage for flower arrangers and send them direct to you—of great value when you are entering competitions or exhibiting.

Some of the street traders both in towns and along the roadside in the country have a wide variety of flowers; at others the choice is limited.

The countryside is almost always a source of plant material, though you must be certain you are not trespassing and that you are permitted to pick from trees and bushes. Many attractive materials for arranging grow in hedgerows; do not take more than you require. Some of this material such as beech leaves and the bracts of the lime tree can be preserved. Fresh plant material that you can collect from the country includes the leaves of the wild arum or cuckoo pint, available in the spring, as are the catkins of the hazel tree. The catkins and small cones of the alder are also interesting and available through the winter. Many different grasses are useful. Wheat and barley may have strayed from the farmer's field and be found in the hedgerow. Find branches with lichen growing on them in damp wet situations, frequently in the west of the British Isles. They are grey in colour and keep well in a cool place for several years. It is best to choose branches which are not too fragile; otherwise they tend to snap, especially those of brittle fir trees. In the autumn, hedgerows produce berries such as the hips, haws and wild guelder rose. The wild clematis is attractive either before or after the seed head becomes fluffy.

Carpet or bun moss, found in woods and damp places, is worth collecting as a cover for the netting in a container; bunches of flowers can also be placed at intervals between it. Keep it moist by spraying overhead; and when it is not in use, keep it out of doors. Lichen moss which often grows under the heather on mountains and moorlands is stored dry. When required soak it until it becomes spongy.

Often you can find interestingly shaped pieces of driftwood on beaches and shores of lochs and lakes. If you have purchased them, they are generally bleached. Bare heather stems can be found on mountains and hills where heather has been burnt. Parts of tree roots are also good to use, as are the twisted stems of old ivy plants.

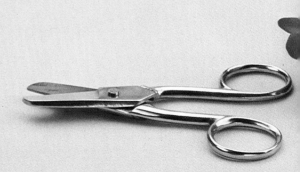

SELECTING PLANT MATERIAL

When beginning flower arranging it is difficult to know how much plant material to use in a container. Knowing the quantities comes with practice; hence in the arrangements that follow I have stated the numbers of flowers and foliage and have given guidelines for alternative plant material.

As you select the types of flowers and foliage, a collection in shades of one colour is impressive—whether you are buying from a shop or gathering from the garden. There is an especially wide range of reds. You can choose either the more yellow reds or the more blue reds. On occasion the two together can look fantastic; this combination is often called clashing reds. Pinks can be used in a similar way but are not as dramatic. Selecting the foliage to match can add much to a colour scheme.

When you go to a garden or flower shop to create a mixed flower arrangement, choose an uneven number of at least three different kinds of flowers: one going one way in the container, one the opposite, and the third as the largest through the centre. Try to balance the plant material each side of the vase, and if possible pick flowers and leaves of slightly different shapes: the spiky, the intricate, and the rounded; this variety immediately adds interest to the arrangement. Choose larger flowers for the centre, such as three chrysanthemum blooms, or five roses for a medium-sized arrangement.

Gathering Flowers from the Garden

When you cut foliage from the garden, take care not to spoil the shape of the shrub or tree, but cut it in a way that leaves the plant still attractive. Cut the twig from where it meets the branch, so avoiding ugly stalks on the plant. Roses are best cut just above a leaf, so the leaf is then at the top of the stem.

Often insufficient flowers of one colour are out simultaneously in a garden for an arrangement which blends. Instead choose a well-mixed coloured collection. Lime green is a good colour to include as it adds sharpness. It is surprising how many green flowers grow in the garden; the flower arrangers' favourite Alchemilla mollis is marvellous in such an arrangement but there are many more including nicotiana, zinnia, euphorbia and helleborus. Use yellow as it brings out the colours of other flowers. It is advisable to omit white from the group as one's eye is drawn towards it. If it *is* included, use it near the centre where the eye will go initially and then travel to the rest of the arrangement. Blue is best placed towards the centre, the lighter colours more on the edges.

When gathering from the garden you can either pick a collection of plant material first and then choose the vase, or vice versa, depending on what flowers are available and on what type of container you want to arrange them in. It is best to have a rough idea as to the size of the container they are to be placed in so that you know roughly how many are required. Try to look for appropriately shaped stems; how they curve determines where to place them in an arrangement. Choose some for the right and some for the left. Straighter stems are best for the tallest plant material; they also need to be quite lightweight, so that the arrangement is not top-heavy.

Enhance the flowers with a range of foliage greens: grey-green, yellow-green, blue-green and also variegated greens. Certain greens complement particular colours. Pinks and mauves go with the grey-green, white and yellow are delightful with the lime-greens;

blue is equally attractive with either of these. Orange and red look striking with copper-coloured foliage. But it is fun to experiment with various colours, and you will discover some surprising results.

Many seed heads from the garden can be stored for winter arrangements, including delphinium, lupin and montbretia. Instead of discarding the seed heads, dry them. Some flowers can be specially grown for drying: helichrysum, honesty (Lunaria) and the Chinese lanterns (Physalis). Foliage such as beech leaves can be used fresh or preserved; they should be picked at the beginning of July for preserving. Many leaves from the garden can be preserved—do experiment with a variety. Hydrangea is a good flower to dry, but do not cut it too early in the year; the insignificant flower in the centre of the bracts should have died. Methods of drying and preserving are explained later (see pages 20–21.)

Buying from the Florist

Buying from the florist you will generally have a wide range of flowers, though (as noted earlier) the foliage could be limited. It is thus relatively easy to achieve a good colour scheme with many varieties of flowers in a wide range of hues—roses, gerbera, carnations, gladioli, chrysanthemums and hyacinths. If you are buying flowers for an arrangement in shades of one colour, you will be able to blend them well and also to choose a good selection of different shapes: the pointed gladiolus, the rounded carnation, a flower with secondary flowers from the main stem such as alstroemeria. Again, where possible, choose a matching foliage.

Check that the flowers you are purchasing look fresh. Buy them preferably while they are still in bud, especially such short-lived flowers as daffodils and roses; you want to take full advantage of them at all stages. Some flowers can be too tightly budded; if they show no colour at the tip of the bud they may never open properly. (Irises are notorious for this.) Gladioli should have one or two of their lower buds opening. Carnations are not very fresh when their stamens are showing above the petals. Chrysanthemums should look fresh at the back of the flowers, without any curled up or fading petals, and the foliage on the stems should look fresh, not droopy. (This is the case with any flower which has foliage growing on its stem.) Multi-headed flowers such as alstroemeria and spray chrysanthemums are good value since you can prune them down and use the flowers separately; select stems which have plenty of flower heads on them—they are useful in a small arrangement where all the flowers can be used individually; in larger arrangements they can be used as one flower.

At the florist's watch for bent or damaged stems and also try to choose those with fairly firm stems for ease in arrangement. Some firm, curved stems are an advantage for the flowers to be used over the edge of the container. In winter it is better not to buy flowers which have been placed in buckets outside the shop as frost may have caught them and consequently they will not keep. See that they are well wrapped against the cold when you take them home. Buy foliage with firm leaves and a good colour, not yellow around the edges. Most florists stock eucalyptus; it keeps for several weeks. There are several varieties, and its grey-green colour makes it especially pretty with pink, blue and mauve flowers. It can also be preserved with glycerine.

Buying dried flowers you must check that they are not mouldy, that the stems are not damaged by being crushed or bent, and that the flower petals are not shattering. (This often happens with helichrysum when it has been gathered too late in the season.) Some dried flowers come without stems and have to be mounted onto florists' stub wires.

Gathering Plant Material from the Countryside
When gathering material from the hedgerow the same care should be taken as when cutting from the garden. Make sure you do not damage the hedge or cut too much from one spot and thus leave a bald patch. Take some damp tissues with you to wrap round the ends of the stems and then place them in a large polythene bag to keep them fresh as you travel home.

CARE OF PLANT MATERIAL

Whether you are gathering from garden or country-side or bringing them home from the florist, all flowers and foliage need general treatment prior to arranging. Remove the lower leaves from the stems and recut the stems before giving them a drink in a deep bucket of tepid water for at least two hours and preferably overnight. This is especially important when plants are cut from the garden or countryside; bought materials have probably been given a long drink by the florist. To make certain, give even florists' flowers and foliage at least two hours; on the way home they lose a certain amount of moisture. Flowers keep so much better in a container when they are already full of water—even when the container is shallow and the stems not far in the water. It is advisable to remove the thorns of roses, though this has probably been done if you have bought them from a florist; the thorns tend to tear the leaves so that you cannot use them

All plant stems need to be cut at an angle at the end. If cut straight across, the stem could rest on the bottom of the container and seal itself, unable to take up any water. This would not happen, of course, with the point of the angle touching the base of the container. Also, a slightly larger surface area when the stem is cut at an angle makes water absorption marginally easier. Angle-cutting the stems is usually sufficient for soft-stemmed flowers, particularly plentiful in the spring and including daffodils, hyacinth and tulips. Harder stems such as sprays of blossom, chrysanthemums and many foliages need to be split at the end of the stem for approximately 25mm/1 inch after they have been cut at an angle. Alternatively hammer with a wooden mallet up to 25–50mm/1–2 inches from the end of the stem both before the initial drink and also when arranging them. Several stems may be hammered at once. Some woody-stemmed flowers and foliage such as lilac and guelder rose need additional treatment: scrape the bark from the end of the stem for 75–100mm/3–4 inches to make a larger surface area for water absorption. If the plant material has notches or nodes at intervals up its stem, cut just above rather than below these to help the stems take up water more easily.

Some plants such as euphorbia and poppy whose stems contain a milky substance will keep better in water if a flame is briefly held at the end of the stem. Use a match, candle or gas flame. Other flowers such as the dahlia also benefit from this treatment as they have a colourless fluid in their stem. After treatment place them in tepid water. Dahlias can also gain from hot water treatment, which is explained on page 19.

Some flowers are susceptible to wilting; hellebore, cyclamen and polyanthus all fall into this category. To aid them, make a shallow slit with a knife into the stem about 25mm/1 inch from the end of the stem and for about 25mm/1 inch. Certain flowers such as violets and hydrangeas take a large amount of water through their petals; a fine mist spray is therefore advantageous, and for their initial drink they can be placed headfirst into the water. It is best to submerge young fresh foliage and ferns for their long drink before arranging them.

Tulips are notorious for not staying straight, as they always bend towards the light; but it does help if you roll them tightly in greaseproof or waxed paper to keep the stems straight until you arrange them. This treatment also helps to keep roses from opening too quickly when you give them their initial drink. Roses which are hothouse-grown, however, often wilt in an arrangement even when they have had the correct treatment prior to arrangement. Should this happen, remove the roses from the container and cover the heads with a polythene bag or tissue paper to protect them. Boil about 25mm/1 inch of water in a pan; place the end of the stems into it for 15–20 seconds. Remove and place them in a container of tepid water so that the water goes most of the way up the stems. The roses should revive unless they have been left too long beforehand.

Often plant material has rather too much foliage that obscures the flowers and berries; consequently, the colour is lost from the arrangement. Philadelphus and leycesteria among many other berried plants are examples. Remove some of the leaves from around the flowers and berries; this also helps the water to reach the flowers and reduces the likelihood of wilting. It is more natural to leave some of the leaves on the stem; but in some cases such as lilac and forced guelder rose (Viburnum opulus), clear the stem completely of foliage; otherwise the flowers wilt because the leaves obtain all the water before it reaches the flower. The leaves can be placed separately in the arrangement. A few of the leaves of the garden guelder rose can be left on.

To stop hollow-stemmed flowers from twisting at the top (for example lupin and eremurus), fill the stem carefully with water, avoiding an air lock, and plug the end with cotton wool or florists' foam. When using a hollow-stemmed flower like the amaryllis, which has very large flower heads on a thick stem, fill the stem with water; to stop the stem from breaking, place a thin cane inside the stem. Then plug the end and tie it with string at the base to hold it in position.

When you use flowers with several flowers growing from the stem, opening from the lower to the upper (such as gladiolus and freesia), you want them to open more quickly if they are tightly budded. Take one or two of the top buds out and the lower ones will open more quickly.

Remove any leaves which go below the water line. Clean stems will keep the water relatively fresh; whereas leaves in water quickly decompose and make the water rather unpleasant. Take away damaged and insect-eaten leaves, using them only when there are not sufficient good ones, low in the arrangement where they will not be noticed. Before arranging the flowers, fill the container three-quarters full of water—never right to the top—since the water level will rise when the stems are placed into the vase. When the arrangement is completed, top up the water if necessary. Check the water level twice a day at first; the flowers drink more water when freshest; afterwards check once each day. Top up with tepid water; the water in the container will become fairly warm and a sudden change of temperature gives the flowers a shorter life. Avoid placing the arrangement in direct sunlight, by a radiator, or by a fire.

Preserving Plant Material

When preserving plant material for the winter you need to carry out various methods of treatment earlier in the year. It has already been treated if bought from the florist, although some fresh materials can be bought and dried. Some flowers dry very easily in an airy place, providing it is not damp so that they go mouldy. Collect seed heads and grasses from the garden and hedgerow. Tie them together in small bunches and hang them upside down. Other flowers such as hydrangea will dry effectively with their stems in about 50mm/2 inches of water; leave them until the bracts become papery. Only use hydrangeas when the small flowers in the centre of the bracts have finished flowering; otherwise they will shrivel. Certain hydrangeas turn different colours: pale pinks generally turn green or if dried in sunlight an attractive shade of pale brown; the darker colours turn mauve and maroon. Outdoor hydrangeas dry more easily than the pot plants, which—being more delicate—tend to go soft.

Beech, eucalyptus, the bracts of the lime tree—among many other leaves—may be preserved with glycerine. Remove the leaves from lime branches so that the attractive bracts can be seen. Cut the foliage when firm but not too near the autumn (when the leaves will drop). Cut beech at the beginning of July. Lime needs to be treated when the flower buds attached to the bracts are about to open; if fully open they tend to look untidy and can become shrivelled. Choose eucalyptus from the garden or flower shop that has not new growth but firm leaves. After gathering the foliage, hammer the ends of the stems and give them a short drink of water in a deep bucket. Next place them in an upright pot or jar with a solution of one-third glycerine to two-thirds hot water—the mixture coming 75mm–100mm/3–4 inches up in the container. Leave for approximately one week, until the leaves or bracts have changed colour. Beech and lime bracts go to a golden shade; the eucalyptus will be darker. If the flowers are left too long in the solution, the oil will come to the surface of the leaves. Antifreeze can be used instead of glycerine and results in a slightly different colour. Many plant materials can be preserved with glycerine and antifreeze; it is worth experimenting with most foliages.

An alternative method for drying eucalyptus is in a small amount of water, as for hydrangea. Bracken and ferns can be dried when placed for a few weeks between newspapers that absorb the moisture and flattened beneath a weight. Under a carpet is ideal.

Other methods of preserving flowers are with either borax or silica gel. For borax, use a mixture of two parts borax and one part silver sand. Place the flowers carefully in a cardboard box so that they do not touch each other, and sprinkle the mixture around them. Gerbera, alchillea, dahlias and roses are suitable. For the silica gel method, use a polythene bag and place the flowers on a layer of silica gel so that they do not touch each other. Put in more silica gel to fill the bag, making sure it goes between the petals. Seal the bag and hang it in a warm place for approximately a week. When the flowers are dried,

carefully remove the silica gel. Store the flowers in a polythene bag with a few crystals until you require them for an arrangement. Again, it is well worth experimenting with a variety of flowers and foliage from the garden.

Lichen branches, unlike many discussed so far, are best stored in bunches in a *cool* place.

COLOUR, SHAPE AND TEXTURE IN THEIR SETTING

Just as there are personal preferences for decorating and furnishing a home, so you will have your own tastes as you choose a flower arrangement for its colour, shape and texture in relation to its room setting. Some ideas follow to help you decide about your arrangements. You want your flowers to complement, not clash with, their surroundings. In a sitting room they are more noticeable on lower tables or in similar positions; in an entrance hall they are better placed higher, near eye level. When matching and blending flowers with a room—not only by coordinating colours, but also by choice of shape and texture of the arrangement—take into consideration the type of room (contemporary, traditional, cottage, or town house), where it is to be situated, and the materials which furnish the room.

A major consideration in determining the colours is whether the room is light or dark. Obviously, certain colours tend to disappear in poor or artificial light. Blue is the colour which shows least in a poorly lit room; hence any colour containing blue also shows up less, depending on the degree of blue. Colours containing blue are purple, mauve, and some pinks, as well as such reds as magenta. All these are best avoided in poor lighting. Instead use yellowish pinks such as salmon-pink and yellowish reds such as coral. Orange flowers are good; yellow and white stand out well from a distance in a large hall or church. If blue and white *are* together in an arrangement, try not to use blue on the main outline points; it would probably not show up, and the arrangement would appear to be an odd shape. Dark churches are particularly problematic for blue.

Colours taken from the room—from curtains, carpets, upholstery, wallpaper and pictures—are more attractive for an arrangement. You have many alternatives to choose from: just one colour taken from the curtain, or a mixture; just one type of flower if the room is elaborately furnished will make the arrangement more restful. A green arrangement rarely clashes with anything and has a cool look for summer. A room decorated in many plain colours is brightened by a large arrangement of mixed flowers in shades of one colour or a mixture of colours. If you place more than one arrangement in a room, it looks most tranquil in the same colour, although one vase could be mixed and the other in just one variety (or another mixture in the same colours). A colour scheme can also be used in a church, the colours perhaps taken from the stained glass windows; but remember where possible to use lighter colours if the arrangement stands in a dark position.

The shape of the arrangement depends on its place in the room. If against a wall, an arrangement to be seen from the front is required; when placed on a table to be seen from all sides, a table centre, all-round, or simple line arrangement that looks equally good from any side is required. On the whole, an elegant room calls for a more traditional arrangement such as a facing arrangement in an urn or an all-round tazza; the stems of these containers immediately make them look graceful. The contemporary room may call for a modern container with arrangements of simple flowers, though not necessarily garden types: for a cylinder container, a flat trough or plate for pinholder arrangements of a few flowers and branches. A cottage home with many nooks and crannies calls for facing arrangements that can be situated in baskets and copper or brass jugs, for small arrangements in china vases on tables and bedside tables. In town houses where furnishings vary, the shape will depend on the style of the furnishing, and where it is to be placed. The arrangement for the dining room should be visible from all sides, low or on a candlestick or candelabrum, so as not to block the view across the table.

If there is a picture or mirror, place an arrangement on a chest or sideboard below it, completed in an L-shape, and framing two sides of the picture or mirror. Under a picture, choose colourings for the flowers that are already in the picture, either mixed or one colour. In the case of a mirror, it is lovely to see the reflection of the flowers and leaves. If a room has a very high ceiling, avoid a tall, slender arrangement. Make it more solid with a somewhat wide facing arrangement, not as high as usual; a tall, thin arrangement would only draw your eyes upward and accentuate the height of the ceiling.

Choosing the textures of both containers and flowers, take into account the materials in the room. Plain and fine materials are complemented by delicate glass and china vases and florists' flowers such as hot-house roses, bridal gladioli, carnations, lilies and freesia. China containers in pastel colours or silver

complement light-coloured furniture; whereas the darker-coloured leather upholstery looks good with brass, copper, pottery, and brighter shades of flowers. Modern print curtains in cotton look cheerful with brightly coloured plastic or pottery containers filled with flowers of the simple daisy type such as single spray chrysanthemums to either match or contrast with the furnishings. Tweed upholstery,

hessian wallpaper and woven curtains would all look splendid with basketwork, copper, brass and rough pottery filled with garden flowers such as marigolds, chrysanthemums, dahlias and daffodils, or with twigs and plants from the hedgerow. Velvet upholstery calls for more traditional arrangements in urns and tazzas made of various metals in colours appropriate to the room.

FACING ARRANGEMENT OF ONE KIND OF FLOWER

Plant Material

12 red chrysanthemum blooms
15 short stems of preserved eucalyptus (see methods of preserving, pages 20–21)

Container

A medium–sized, dark green tazza, a small square of florists' foam beneath 50-mm/2-inch mesh wire netting (see page 9)

Creating the Arrangement

This is a basic symmetrical facing arrangement. Begin by placing the six main outline points to give you guidance for the size and shape of the arrangement. These six points consist of three flowers, each a slightly different length, which serve as the tallest flowers; a flower on either side of the container to determine the width; and a flower coming out in the centre of the vase at the front edge, to show the longest point to work to at the front. These six flowers form the main outline. In a basic facing arrangement the height is approximately the same as the overall width.

For the tallest chrysanthemums at the back choose a small flower with relatively long stem since the height of the arrangement should be at least one-and-a-half times the height of the container. (This applies when the vase has a stem.) A second chrysanthemum with slightly larger flower and about a head shorter than the first goes to the left of it, and a third chrysanthemum, slightly larger still but a head shorter than the second, goes to the right of the first flower. These three flowers should be relatively close together and positioned three-quarters of the way back in the centre of the tazza. Insert them through the netting into the florists' foam to establish them firmly. Next go to the flowers for the widest points, choosing smaller flowers but saving the very smallest for the front edge. Place the two side chrysanthemums horizontally, three-quarters back in the tazza, remembering the proportions of the arrangement. The last outline flower, the one at the front, goes low against the rim in the centre of the container, coming well out at the front so that a semi-circle can be formed between the widest points around the front edge of the tazza.

At this stage it is helpful to put in some of the preserved eucalyptus to cover part of the wire netting and a few of the flower stems. The leaves on the chrysanthemum stems should be left on unless they go beneath the water line or are too heavily foliaged to be attractive. Position the remaining six chrysanthemum blooms. Keeping the largest two for the centre, place one on either side towards the outline at the back, remembering they should not be longer than the main outline points; each should be a different length. Place one on either side of the longest flower at the front, at different lengths and levels. Place the two remaining flowers near the centre, one low into the arrangement and one a little higher to give height in the centre. All the flowers should be evenly distributed in the container, keeping as many different levels as possible, even though the flowers are large and there are only twelve. Finish the arrangement by putting more eucalyptus sprays where necessary, placing a few at the back behind the main outline flowers to cover the quarter of the tazza not used. (If flowers began right at the back of the tazza it would be too large an area to fill, and you would finish with a bulging arrangement instead of an elegant shape.) Check the water is to the rim of the container.

Alternative Plant Material

18 yellow gerbera; the flowers are smaller than chrysanthemums so a greater number is needed.
15 croton leaves, in yellow shades cut from a pot plant.

Many varieties of flowers are useful for this type of flower arrangement: among them *roses, carnations, arum lilies, anthuriums, iris, tulips and peonies.*

The flowers with a single head on a stem are best.

Alternative Containers

A copper bowl or tazza would be ideal for the chrysanthemums. When using other flowers and colours, possible containers would include metal tazzas and bowls, troughs, urns and cylinders of various colours. The arrangement does look particularly pleasing in a container with a stem.

Occasion

An arrangement for the autumn and winter, it would last well in a home, office or church; chrysanthemums are long-lasting flowers. As it is a facing arrangement place it in a niche or on a side table where the back of the arrangement would not be seen.

FACING ARRANGEMENT OF MIXED FLOWERS

Plant Material

11 mauve liatris
7 pink carnations
5 mauve spray chrysanthemums
7 blue iris
3 stems spiraea
9 stems fuchsia foliage
11 stems pink-berried snowberry
11 stems santolina foliage
9 stems rue (Ruta graveolens) foliage
3 bergenia leaves

Container

A grey pottery tazza with a pinholder placed in it and 50-mm/2-inch mesh wire netting placed over it (see page 9)

Creating the Arrangement

This symmetrical facing arrangement has six main outline points as does the basic facing arrangement just described. Before starting to arrange mixed flowers and mixed colours, decide how best the types and colours of flowers should be placed for a balanced arrangement. In this collection of flowers and foliage, the large number of pointed liatris can be grouped with the lesser number of spiraea and snowberry, and with the rue foliage. Group them from high on the right to low on the left. As there are fewer chrysanthemums, the carnations assist this group with the santolina and fuchsia foliage. The foliage being all grey and the fuchsia also containing pink blend well with the other colours. The main flowers for the centre are blue iris which come through the centre, beginning to the right of the tallest flower at the top and finishing to the left of the longest flower over the front edge. Keep bergenia leaves central so that they and the iris establish a focal point. Begin the arrangement with a fairly small and long-stemmed liatris, placing it through the wire netting into the pinholder, three-quarters of the way back in the tazza in a central position; it should be at least one-and-a-half times the height of the container. Next place a second (larger-flowered but a little shorter) liatris to the right of the first liatris as the second flower. A third flower, a fairly small spray chrysanthemum with a relatively long stem, is placed to the left of the first liatris and has a little shorter stem than the second liatris. If the chrysanthemum flower head is too large, a few flowers can be removed and used later low in the arrangement to give depth. These three stems are quite close together to give a pointed top to the arrangement; they could even be placed through the same hole in the netting.

Now go to the widest points; on the left place a liatris and on the right a spray chrysanthemum with a few flowers removed to make it balance with the opposite side. Place both flowers horizontally over the rim of the tazza, three-quarters of the way back in it, gauging the overall width to be approximately the height. The longest flower in the centre at the front edge is a small liatris, long enough to enable flowers to come well out around the front edge and connect flowers with container to make a complete unit.

The main flowers, the iris, are placed next using smaller flowers at the top and over the front edge, but keeping the largest ones nearer the centre. Place one iris fairly high towards the back of the arrangement, one to the left of the longest flower on the front edge; make it a little shorter. Place the other five iris; working on either side from the tallest at the top to the one at the front edge, zigzag them through the tazza getting progressively nearer the centre on either side until you reach the centre. Vary the stem length as shown in the first picture of the arrangement. Place the three bergenia leaves in position, one over the front edge on the right side, one turning sideways left

of centre, and one facing towards the front but placed near the back of the arrangement, slightly left of centre. Place some foliage on either side, remembering to group correctly—some pieces high and some low.

The first picture shows where the plant material groups are, with the main outline flowers and the focal point. Now go to the periphery and continue going down at the sides, decreasing stem lengths quite quickly with more flowers in their appropriate groups and maintaining the shape. Create a broken rather than a solid line and make an irregular look around the edges, both along the back and round the front. When the outline flowers are in position, place more flowers throughout the arrangement. Where possible the smaller-headed flowers should be longer to build up the arrangement from the longest around the front edge to the tallest flower at the back. When you look at it from the side, it should still be a triangular shape. Larger flowers are kept lower, but still remember to keep to the correct groups. Merge the groups around the centre of the container where they cross from one side to the other. Do not forget the stems which are in-between lengths; cut stem lengths with plenty of variation. Place more foliage attractively throughout the arrangement in the appropriate groups, making sure the wire netting is covered. Some leaves curve over the rim of the tazza. Short-stemmed pieces cover the quarter of the container left at the back of the arrangement. The tazza should contain sufficient water for all the stems to be under the water line.

This arrangement creates an analogous colour scheme; that is, you are using one particular colour and adding to it the colour from either side of it on the colour wheel. This technique is useful when you are unable to obtain flowers in shades of one colour.

Alternative Plant Material

7 scarlet gladioli
7 orange-red antirrhinums
9 blue-red roses
11 blue-red dahlias
5 red anthuriums
3 Mahonia bealei leaves
15 stems flowering cherry foliage
11 stems autumnal coloured peony leaves

This collection would make a clashing red group; it is great fun used at a party and always makes a good talking point, whether it is liked or disliked!

Alternative Containers

A pewter tazza would blend well with this arrangement of pink, mauve and blue; it would also look splendid with the clashing red flowers. Other containers suitable for a facing arrangement are bowls, urns, tazzas and troughs in various coloured china and pottery; metal vases such as copper, brass and silver and basketwork containers.

Occasion

The arrangement would be suitable in size and shape for a party and could be used as a small pedestal group. Because blue is used, the lighting should be quite good; but a blue does not outline the arrangement, the shape would not be spoiled if the iris did not show up as well as the other flowers. Designed to be seen from the front, this arrangement should be set against a wall or other background.

ASYMMETRICAL FACING ARRANGEMENT

Plant Material

3 sprays cream orchids
6 stems apricot spray carnations
5 stems cream spray carnations
9 yellow freesia
1 orange lily
5 stems golden privet (Ligustrum) foliage
9 stems variegated ivy (Hedera) foliage
7 stems yellow-green euonymous foliage
4 stems autumn-tinged summer jasmine
   (Jasminum officinale) foliage
3 croton leaves cut from a pot plant

Container

A white china dolphin with a shell; inside, a rectangular piece of florists' foam with a small piece of 50-mm/2-inch mesh wire netting over it, tied in with silver reel wire that goes around the dolphin's tail as seen in the first picture of the arrangement.

Creating the Arrangement

As does a symmetrical facing arrangement, the asymmetrical has six main outline points, though these are not all placed in the same positions. The highest point comes to the right side of this dolphin container, approximately a quarter of the way from the side edge and three-quarters of the way back in the container, following the line of the dolphin's tail. Because of the shell, which is low and spreading, the arrangement need not be one-and-a-half times the height of the vase but kept lower and wider. For this reason, the height is not the same as the overall width.

Determine the groups of plant material before beginning the arrangement, to make sure of a balanced arrangement: the orchids, apricot spray carnations (used as individual flowers), golden privet and ivy going high on the right to low on the left; the cream spray carnation (again used individually), freesia, euonymous and jasmine foliage going the opposite way. The head of lily and the croton leaves are the focal point in the centre.

The orchid is used as the tallest flower as it is light in colour and weight with creamy, green buds at the top. A bud of the cream carnation a little shorter than the orchid stands on its left side, and an apricot carnation bud a little shorter than the second flower stands to the right of the tallest flower. These are all fairly close together, three-quarters of the way back in the shell, and about a quarter of the way in from the right side. The widest flowers on the sides are placed next: on the left an orchid spray coming low and quite long-stemmed, placed three-quarters back in the container and following its natural curve. On the right side, and in the same line in the dolphin vase, a freesia about half the length of the orchid curves out. The longest flower over the front is a cream carnation bud and goes in the same line as the tallest orchid at the back, though not in the centre of the front rim. It should not be too long since some of the dolphin should show in the completed arrangement. For this reason the flowers and leaves all along the front edge are shorter than in a basic facing arrangement.

Once the six principal points are in position, the focal point is placed next—the orange lily to give weight to the centre. (Three or five larger flowers could be used instead.) The lily is quite short, placed in a central position with the three croton leaves around it: one over the left edge at the front, the biggest turning sideways to the right of the centre, and the third facing towards the front but placed behind the lily and in the same line as the first croton leaf. Next place some foliage to help cover the wire netting and florists' foam and also some in the outline to show the grouping. Remember to arrange the

jasmine and euonymous high on the left to low on the right, and the ivy and privet the opposite way. Place a few of the leaves higher in the container. The first picture of the arrangement shows this stage.

Go to the periphery and place flowers between the main outline points, keeping an uneven line. Keep it reasonably light along the front edge. Decrease the stem lengths quite quickly on the back outline to keep an attractive shape. Arrange more flowers throughout the vase keeping the buds, small flowers and daintier leaves higher, and the heavier material lower; merge the groups through the centre. Build the flowers up from the front edge to the tallest flowers at the back, being careful not to make them longer than the outline flowers and so spoil the shape. The focal point should not be too obvious, so choose a few lightweight plant materials higher than the lily. The stems need to radiate or look as if they are growing from the tallest flowers at the back. Do not place the flower and leaf stems too far into the container, or it will be difficult to place all stems into position when the arrangement is nearly completed. Avoid placing two flowers beside each other of the same stem length, but vary them to obtain a more interesting arrangement.

Check that the florists' foam and wire netting is hidden with the small pieces of foliage and short flowers, and that some foliage and flowers are placed at the back of the vase behind the outline flowers. If necessary top up the container with water to the rim to make sure all the stems are under the water line. Cut away the reel wire holding the netting into the vase, as when all the plant material is positioned it should be balanced and stable.

Alternative Plant Material

9 stems pink escallonia
5 stems white alstroemeria, used as individual flowers
5 white pinks (dianthus)
9 white sweet pea (Lathyrus odoratus)
5 pale pink roses
15 stems periwinkle (Vinca) foliage
11 stems hebe foliage
3 small ferns

Alternative Container

Instead of the dolphin vase an ornate wrought-iron container would be suitable. Usually such vases have a small, round container at the top to hold the flowers. In other colour schemes there is a range of containers which are shallow and rest on a stem; they may be china or metal. The china Cupid vases are also a good shape for the asymmetrical facing arrangement.

Occasion

Use the arrangement as a buffet vase at a christening party or wedding reception, especially when the reception is held at home; it is not too large. If for a wedding, choose the colour for the flowers from the colours of the bride's or bridesmaids' dresses. This shape of arrangement is suitable in a pair: one with its height on one side and the other on the opposite side. It would be ideal for the top table.

A SIMPLE LINE ARRANGEMENT

Plant Material

5 stems of white silk poppies: each stem contains 1 flower, 1 bud and 2 leaves

Accessory
3 small marble pebbles

Container
A stainless steel tray with a medium-sized pinholder which has a small square of dry florists' foam on it.

Creating the Arrangement
Use the pinholder with the dry florists' foam on it three-quarters of the way back and in a central position on the tray. Preferably use a heavy-based pinholder; otherwise attach a lighter one to the tray with Bostik Blu-tack or a similar substance; this will hold the flowers more firmly.

Silk flowers can be made different sizes by pushing the petals, which have wires in them, either closer together or wider apart. The stems also have wires in them and can be gently curved to the required position. The stems should be cut for a successful arrangement; if you need them longer for another arrangement, make false stems with florists' stub wires.

Begin the arrangement by placing a small flower as the tallest flower, its stem slightly longer than the width of the tray, three-quarters of the way back in a central position on the dry florists' foam. Leave a bud at the side if it has one; this poppy has one on the left.

Choose a second flower a little more open and about a head shorter and place it to the right of the first, fractionally forward on the pinholder. Take the buds and leaves from it to be used later. Where possible cut the buds and leaves with as much stem on them as possible. A third flower larger still and approximately a head shorter than the second flower is placed on the left side of the tallest poppy, again more forward on the pinholder and dry florists' foam. Place a bud on either side of the arrangement, to keep it light on the sides, for the widest points; they are three-quarters back and low on the dry foam. The longest point on the front edge is another bud placed in the centre, close to the tray. Put in a few leaves at this stage, to cover the pinholder and dry foam, some over the tray to connect the flowers and leaves with the container. If the leaf stem is not sufficiently long, a false stem can be put on it. A fourth and more open poppy, shorter than the third flower, is placed to the side of the second flower. The fifth and largest flower is low towards the centre of the arrangement. The remaining bud is between the fourth and fifth poppies and any remaining leaves are positioned, some covering some of the flower stems, the rest arranged attractively through the flowers.

Complete the arrangement by placing three pieces of marble on the tray: the two larger pieces are placed nearer to the pinholder to help cover it and to add weight nearer the centre of the arrangement; the smallest piece of marble is placed nearer the edge of the tray, to balance the leaf placed low on the right of the centre bud. Stand away from the arrangement to see if it looks pleasing at all angles.

Alternative Plant Material
Fresh plant material is equally attractive in a line arrangement and flowers which could be used are *5 pink peonies with their own foliage*. A small container would be required to hold the water and pinholder.

Alternative Accessory
Pink pebbles to match the flowers.

Alternative Containers
For the white silk poppies a flat marble plate would be ideal. If you choose other coloured plant material, use brass, copper, silver and pewter trays or plates; also wickerwork and wooden platters and trays; or porcelain plates and dishes—pick up the colours from them with the flowers.

Occasion
A gift for a silver wedding present. It is also a useful arrangement for the home, even against a radiator.

ALL-ROUND ARRANGEMENT OF ONE KIND OF FLOWER

Plant Material

50 blue brodiaea
**7 stems variegated euonymous foliage cut into
  sprigs**
5 medium-sized variegated ivy leaves

Container
An off-white bowl with a blue decoration; a square
of florists' foam with 50-mm/2-inch mesh wire
netting over it is placed inside (see pages 9–10)

Creating the Arrangement
To obtain a round shape for the basic all-round
arrangement, it is better to begin with the principal
outline points around the edge of the bowl. An
uneven number is better, as it is less likely to look too
rigid. The number you choose varies with the size of
the bowl and the number of flowers available. This
container measures 200mm/8 inches in diameter; I
have seven outline points. The flowers on the outline
all need to be the same length from the rim of the
bowl to their tips, and approximately equal distance
apart. Place the flowers well over the rim so that the
container and plant material become a unit. Use the
smaller brodiaea, the ones with the least number of
flowers on each stem, and those in bud. When the
seven flowers are established around the edge, with
stems going about half way towards the centre of the
bowl, place the tallest flower in the centre; this is a
small one. The height should be roughly the overall
width. If the vase has a stem and is for a table centre, it
would be lower. Around the tallest flower are three
or four flowers of varying lengths, placed quite close
together.

Next go to the outline edge and place flowers of
various length between the main outline points,

avoiding a circle within a circle and also a star shape; instead, create a broken line. At this stage arrange some euonymous foliage to cover some of the netting, to go around the outline, and a few in the centre. The five ivy leaves when in position give a more solid look: a smaller one goes over the edge of either side, a slightly larger one nearer the centre on either side and to one side of the first two ivy leaves, and the largest leaf turning sideways in the centre of the bowl. Thus ivy leaves zigzag from one side to the other. Gradually build up the arrangement with flowers and leaves from the outline edge to the centre flowers, using stems of varying lengths. Short, larger flowers and leaves are needed to give depth. Too much foliage, however, looks untidy. Check the water level, and cut away the silver wire which ties the wire netting in the bowl.

Alternative Plant Material
60 white (with blue centres) dimorphotheca
5 grey-green geranium leaves
15 stems grey hebe foliage cut into sprigs

Alternative Containers
A blue or white tazza. Any shallow bowl, tazza, round dish with or without a stem or round basket, depending on the colour and type of plant material: for example pink or white sweet peas in a silver bowl.

Occasion
A table centre for a round table at a luncheon party, as the blue flowers would not show up in artificial light. It is also suitable for a wedding reception when the bridesmaids are wearing blue.

The arrangement is photographed from above.

ALL-ROUND ARRANGEMENT OF MIXED FLOWERS (PASTELS)

Plant Material

5 cream spray carnations
7 pink spray carnations
9 mauve freesia
5 stems pink Viburnum fragrans
9 stems yellow winter jasmine (Jasminum nudiflorum)
9 blue brodiaea
3 pink roses
9 stems green budded heather (Erica)
3 stems rue (Ruta graveolens) foliage
5 stems trailing ivy (Hedera) foliage
9 stems golden privet (Ligustrum)
5 single ivy leaves

Container

A shallow glass on a stem; half a round of florists' foam with a single layer of 50-mm/2-inch mesh wire netting over it, tied in with silver reel wire (see pages 9–10)

Creating the Arrangement

The arrangement has been photographed in four stages using identical glasses to show how it has been achieved. As in the case of the basic all-round of one flower, an uneven number of flowers is required for the outline; this one needs seven, a smaller one five. Do not use three as this would make it triangular; a larger bowl can have nine, eleven and so on. As it is a mixed arrangement, the grouping has to be taken into consideration. If you use two of one kind of flower on the outline, one goes on one side and the other on the opposite side. If you use three, two would go beside each other on one side, forming a double group, and one on the opposite side. If you use four, have a double group on either side. When only one flower is used, the flowers go towards the opposite side but do not quite reach the main outline.

In this arrangement the seven outline flowers, which are small ones or buds, are—in a clockwise direction—mauve freesia, pink carnation, blue brodiaea, yellow jasmine, pink carnation, green-budded heather and cream carnation. When the flowers are sufficiently long and not too large, it is advisable to introduce each of the varieties of the outline. As there are only three roses for the main flowers, they are better nearer the centre. The five viburnum are grouped with the freesia. The principal outline flowers are placed as the all-round of brodiaea. The tallest flower in the centre is a cream carnation bud, with a freesia, brodiaea, pink carnation and heather around it—as the first picture of the arrangement shows. Place some foliage to show the grouping: the golden privet with the cream carnations and the brodiaea; the rue with mauve freesia and jasmine; the ivy with the pink carnation. Each foliage group merges with the one beside it. The second picture shows the arrangement at this stage.

The third picture shows more flowers around the

outline edge and throughout the arrangement, placed as for the all-round of brodiaea. Remember to group the plant material properly. The three roses are placed in: one on each side near the rim and the largest in the centre, but they are not in a straight line. The five variegated ivy leaves are placed through with the roses as in the brodiaea arrangement. Position the plant material throughout the arrangement, varying stem lengths. Merge each group with the one beside it, so avoiding slices of colour round the container. Check that the "mechanics" are covered with leaves, and make sure the florists' foam is kept wet.

Alternative Plant Material

7 small red Euphorbia fulgens
11 red anemones
3 red spray chrysanthemums, the flowers used
    individually
7 small red roses
7 red coloured buds of skimmia
9 green trailing ivy
5 stems berried holly
a red candle for the centre
    for a Christmas
    arrangement

Alternative Container

A shallow silver bowl. For other colours and types of flowers any round container with or without a stem. A candlecup on a candlestick would be suitable, but the arrangement should be kept low.

Occasion

An ideal gift for someone in hospital or unwell at home, it is a good size for a bedside table.

A SIMPLE ALL-ROUND ARRANGEMENT

Plant Material (all taken from pot plants)

7 stems asparagus fern
5 begonia leaves with brown markings
7 scindapsus leaves
7 stems trailing ivy (Hedera)
5 stems maidenhair fern
5 leaves fern (Pteris)
an interestingly shaped piece of wood

Container

A round wooden board with a small, round metal dish on it, in which there is a heavy pinholder with florists' foam on top

Creating the Arrangement

Choose an attractively shaped piece of wood—this is part of a bare stem of bracken—and leave it in its natural state. Firmly establish the wood—this is in one piece—and place it onto the florists' foam and through to the pinholder. Thin-stemmed pot plants would be difficult to establish on a pinholder, but the pinholder *is* required to give weight under the florists' foam for the piece of wood. Put the tallest piece of plant material—this is an asparagus fern—in the centre just below the highest piece of wood. The different plant materials go from one side of the arrangement to the opposite, as in an all-round arrangement.

The nine outline points go round the edge to determine the shape, which should be round, in keeping with the wooden board but not as formal as a basic all-round previously illustrated; parts of the board should show to add interest to the arrangement. The principal outline points are two maidenhair fern, two ivy, one scindapsus leaf, two fern and two asparagus fern. Having only one scindapsus on the outline, go nearly to the edge of the opposite side.

The begonia leaves do not have sufficiently long stems to reach the outline, but they go nearly to it on either side.

The many different types of leaves make a more pleasing arrangement, as do a wide selection of shapes. Place more of the plant material throughout the container, varying the stem lengths and so providing the arrangement with interest. Radiate the stems from the tallest asparagus fern in the centre. Make sure again that the wood is easily visible since it is the focal point. Materials of each kind zigzag from one side to the other; let the sprays arch naturally. The markings on the begonia leaves pick up and match well with the colour of the board. The pinholder and florists' foam should be covered in the completed arrangement. Top up the small container with water and check it frequently.

Alternative Plant Material (from the hedgerow)

7 stems rose hips
7 stems hawthorn berries
9 wild clematis seed heads
7 small ferns or bracken
7 stems green ivy

Alternative Container

A round wickerwork tray. If using coloured flowers, choose other containers such as round trays of brass, copper or silver.

Occasion

A useful arrangement for the home or office, this would last well and would be less expensive than flowers. Suitable for a round table.

TABLE CENTRE OF ONE KIND OF FLOWER

Plant Material

50 daffodils with their leaves (or spikes)
26 sprigs golden privet (Ligustrum) foliage
3 oval bergenia leaves

Container

A rectangular wickerwork basket with a plastic container of the same size placed in it. In the centre of the plastic container place a pinholder with several layers of 50-mm/2-inch mesh wire netting over it, tied in with silver reel wire (see pages 9–10)

Creating the Arrangement

Begin this basic table centre arrangement with the main outline points. First establish the length required on either end by placing three flowers horizontally on either side, well over the edge of the basket; choose smaller-headed flowers for this, with the smallest head and the longest-stemmed in the middle. Place a second slightly larger but shorter-stemmed flower on one side of it, and a third flower (again slightly larger and shorter-stemmed than the second daffodil) on the opposite side of it. Going to the widest points next in a central position on the side edge, place a small daffodil or bud on either side of the container near to and extending slightly over the rim. To finish the placement of the main outline points, put the tallest flower in the centre of the basket, firmly fixed in a pinholder and not too high; choose a bud or small flower for it. For spring flowers it is preferable to use a pinholder and netting as the stems are difficult to get into the florists' foam. Around the tallest flower place two or three daffodils of varying lengths, each progressively larger but shorter-stemmed.

With these principal points in position, place some golden privet through the arrangement together with small bunches of three or five daffodil leaves or spikes. They should not be too long as they tend to look untidy. Both kinds of leaves assist in covering the wire netting; now place some around the edges of the basket. Position the bergenia leaves, the smaller two on each side of the arrangement, near the widest flowers on the side, diagonally opposite each other; they should go over the edge of the basket. Place the largest leaf sideways nearer the centre of the basket, but not in a straight line with the other two.

You will require more daffodils around the edge of the basket; keep them within the main outline flowers to retain the shape, and use smaller flowers. Gradually build up the flowers from both sides and ends to the tallest flowers in the centre. Use the smaller flowers and buds to do this but save the largest daffodils to put lowest in the arrangement for depth.

Place more flowers of various lengths in the basket, carefully interspersing more daffodil spikes and golden privet leaves. Keep turning the basket from side to side to help to distribute the plant material equally over the arrangement. Check that all the stems are below the water line, and that the netting is covered without looking overcrowded; leave spaces for the buds to open.

When you create an arrangement of this shape in mixed flowers, group the flowers diagonally across the container as for the asymmetrical arrangement on pages 46–49.

Alternative Plant Material

10 stems bronze spray chrysanthemum, some flowers taken from the stems and used individually
15 stems copper beech
3 Mahonia aquifolia leaves

Alternative Containers

A brass trough would be perfect for the daffodils. Other containers for this shape of arrangement include copper and pottery troughs, oblong baskets with a handle, oval-shaped containers with or without a stem.

Occasion

Lovely at Easter on a rectangular table where it needs to be seen from all sides. Also suitable for a church arrangement.

ASYMMETRICAL TABLE CENTRE

Plant Material

13 red carnations
15 red roses
5 red apples
12 stems red berried holly
11 stems fir

Accessories

2m/2yd of 50-mm/2-inch red velvet ribbon made into bows

Container

A silver meat cover in a wrought-iron stand; a large oblong of florists' foam is placed in it with 50-mm/ 2-inch mesh wire netting over it, tied into position in four places with silver reel wire (see pages 9–10)

Creating the Arrangement

Begin with the tallest flower, placing it in the centre line of the container approximately a quarter of the way from the side on either side. If you are completing a pair, the highest point would be to the right in one and to the left in the other. In this vase the tallest flower is on the left—a rose. It curves slightly to the left and is not too tall, as the length of the arrangement needs to be greater than its height, because of the shape of the meat cover. Place two or three flowers at different heights around the tallest one, each with a progressively larger head. On the right side of the container—in the centre of it, coming well out over the rim—is a small carnation as the longest point here. A rose a fraction shorter is on one side of it, a carnation shorter still on the other. The longest flower on the left side—approximately half the length of the one on the right, and again near the rim—is a rose. Place it in the middle with a rose on one side of it and a carnation on the other, each a different length. Place the rose diagonally opposite to the rose on the other side of the container, and the carnation diagonally opposite the carnation on the right. These flowers establish the grouping. The widest points on the side of the vase are in line with the tallest flower in the centre, and are low against the rim of the container, a rose one side, a carnation on the other. These are the principal outline points and the grouping can be seen going diagonally through the arrangement.

It is helpful to place the apples and bows fairly early. The apples have four stub wires, two going one way and two going the opposite way, placed through the apple near to its stalk. Twist the wires around each other, then cover them with waterproof tape so that they do not rust in the water. (See the first

picture of the arrangement.) Group the apples with the carnations, the smallest placed near the edge of the container to the left of the rose at the side. Hook the wire from the false stem of the apple into the wire netting, which holds them securely, as the apples are heavy. A larger apple is placed to one side, a little further into the container; the largest apple is nearer the centre. The remaining two apples are positioned in a similar way to the first two, diagonally opposite them in the arrangement. Make the ribbon bows by covering florists' stub wires with strips of red crepe paper; attach the covered wires at the back of the ribbon with sticky tape, then loop the ribbon. Make one bow with just loops and two others with a loop and tail; then see that they are held in position with stub wires. These wires are again covered with crepe

paper and are twisted around the base of the ribbons and then covered with waterproof tape. Place the bows into the arrangement, going the opposite way to the apples and so balancing them; a ribbon with loop and tail goes on either side at the edge of the container. The largest with the three loops goes near the centre of the arrangement.

Place some foliage through the arrangement at this stage: the fir with the carnations, and the holly with the roses. Keep within the main outline points and vary the lengths. Place more flowers throughout the vase, building them up gradually from the sides and ends to the tallest flowers and placing some around the outline edge. Vary the stem length of both flowers and leaves, and radiate the stems from the tallest flower in the centre. Position more holly and fir in the container; and if the leaves of the holly are hiding the berries, remove some of them. There should be approximately the same amount of plant material on either side of the arrangement so that it looks well balanced. Check the netting is covered and that there is sufficient water in the container to cover all the stems.

Alternative Plant Material
9 stems pink flowering cherry
3 stems pink rhododendron
7 stems pink camellia
5 pink peonies
5 hosta leaves
foliage from the flowers
2 bunches of black grapes

Alternative Accessory
2m/2yd of 50-mm/2-inch pink ribbon.
This would be suitable for a girl's 21st birthday party.

Alternative Containers
For the red collection a black Warwick urn. Other containers for different selections are tazzas, shallow dishes on a stem, oval dishes with or without stem and flat bowls.

Occasion
A Christmas arrangement for a table centre at a buffet supper party. A table centre for a dinner party would be completed in the same way but with a lower container.

TABLE CENTRE ARRANGEMENT ON A PINHOLDER

Plant Material

17 pale pink roses (Bridal Pink) with leaves

Accessory
5 blocks of glass

Container
A shallow, oval glass dish with a medium-sized pinholder

Creating the Arrangement
In this arrangement, the placement of flowers is more flexible. Arrange the five blocks of glass attractively round the pinholder, which is in the centre of the dish, before positioning the roses. Then place a small rose firmly in the centre of the pinholder as the tallest flower. It needs sufficient height to allow for variation of stem lengths, but not too high so as to obscure anyone's view across the table. Keep the shape roughly like that of the container. It will be less formally arranged around the edge than the basic table centre, and spaces need to be left where the glass is positioned. Put fairly small roses on either end of the dish and on either side of the arrangement in reasonably central positions. Place a few more flowers around the edge between the pieces of glass. At this stage leaves can go in to cover the pinholder; it is easier to place them in before the roses are in position. If the leaves are not too heavy, keep some on the rose stems.

Build the flowers up towards the highest flower in the centre, arranging some flowers amongst the blocks of glass, and using the whole area of the pinholder for the stems. Push stem ends of the flowers around the edge sideways onto the pinholder. Place smaller roses higher in the arrangement and the larger ones lower. Avoid putting all the flowers on one side before going to the opposite side because you may not have enough flowers left; keep going from side to side all the time so that they are fairly evenly distributed. Put more leaves among the roses before the last of the roses is placed into position. Where possible keep a small piece of flower stem on the leaf to hold it more securely on the pinholder. Check that there is a variety of stem length even though the arrangement is low.

This dish is sufficiently deep for water to cover the pinholder. The water around the glass looks cool and fresh.

Alternative Plant Material
15 white gardenias, with their own foliage.
Many flowers look lovely in this type of arrangement, including *camellia, azalea and clematis*.

Alternative Accessories
Pieces of marble, various coloured pebbles, shells and coral. When blocks of glass are not available, substitute by covering pebbles with silver foil and gluing on to them shattered windscreen glass, which you may be able to get from garages. Use various sized and shaped pebbles in the dish.

Alternative Container
For the roses: a shallow, pale pink, china dish shaped in an oval. For other plant material: any shallow dishes with or without a stem, flat meat plates and oval silver dishes or cake baskets. For these arrangements a smaller container is also needed to hold the water and the pinholder.

Occasion
A summer dinner party. The glass, suggestive of ice, makes the arrangement cool for a hot summer evening. Delicate flowers of one variety also add to this impression.

L-SHAPED ARRANGEMENT

Plant Material

9 white chincherinchee
9 white carnations
3 white gladioli
5 stems white spray chrysanthemum
3 creamy white gerbera
7 stems skimmia foliage, cut into small pieces
7 stems green hebe foliage, cut into smaller
 pieces
3 bergenia leaves

Container

In a white china trough, a pinholder is placed on the left side with several layers of 50-mm/2-inch mesh wire netting is over it, tied in with silver reel wire (see pages 9–10)

Creating the Arrangement

It is easier to place the main outline flower first. These are the three tallest flowers, the widest flower on either side and the longest one over the front edge. These immediately provide a shape and framework for the flowers. A pointed flower is the most suitable to begin with; hence place a gladiolus three-quarters of the way back, as with any facing arrangement, and approximately a quarter of the way from the edge of the container—the side you place it depending on which way the L is required for its situation. The height in this one is on the left.

On the left of the gladiolus, taking into consideration the grouping of the flowers, place a chrysanthemum a little shorter than the gladiolus. If it is too heavy, remove a few flowers, leaving as much stem as possible. Use these later in the arrangement to give depth. As you take them off, try to cut them from the stem so that it is not readily noticeable. Place chincherinchee on the right of the gladiolus, a little shorter still. All three stems should be quite close together and established firmly on the pinholder.

Go to the right of the container and place a gladiolus horizontally, three-quarters of the way back in the trough, coming well away from the side. Go then to the left side and again three-quarters back against the edge of the container; place a chincherinchee horizontally, approximately half the length of the gladiolus on the opposite side. The last of the main outline flowers, the one at the front edge, is a reasonably small chincherinchee, in line with the tallest flower at the back, coming well over the edge so that the rest of the flowers placed around the front rim form a nice sweep from side to side. Now place the most important flowers—the three gerbera—in the vase: a smaller one towards the back of the arrangement, just in front of the tallest flowers already in position, and with about half their length of stem; another coming out over the front edge of the trough to the right of the longest chincherincheree at the front, this being the smaller of the two remaining gerbera; the third and largest gerbera between the first two but to the left of them, so avoiding a straight line. Place the three bergenia leaves against them; one towards the back and facing the front, one under the gerbera at the front edge, and the third and largest going sideways and under the gerbera in the centre. This pattern of flowers and foliage gives weight to the arrangement and forms the focal point.

Some of the other plant material can now be positioned on the periphery, and with the chincherinchee—going high on the right to low on the left—are the carnations and skimmia foliage. With the gladioli and chrysanthemums is the hebe foliage. The first picture of this arrangement shows the positioning up to this stage.

To achieve the shape of the L, the flowers and foliage stems should decrease in length quickly on the right side, but should also vary in stem lengths; the short, longer and in-between ones are still required. Intersperse foliage before all the flowers are in the arrangement; it is easier to cover the netting at this stage. Gradually bring the flowers down on the outline at the back on the left side to meet the widest chincherinchee. Evenly distribute the plant material. Arrange the flowers so that they come well out over the front edge; build the flowers from the longest over the front edge to the tallest flowers at the back, where it is especially necessary to obtain some height. For this purpose the third gladiolus is an ideal flower as its buds make it light, and the smaller flowers are best placed higher.

Check the wire netting is covered, but not crowded, with plant material. The water line should be to the rim of the trough so that all the stems are in water.

Alternative Plant Material

7 stems stripped lime (bracts of lime)
9 stems Euphorbia epithymoides
9 stems Alchemilla mollis
5 stems guelder rose (Viburnum opulus) in green stage
7 Arum italicum
9 stems varigated periwinkle (Vinca)
9 stems evergreen honeysuckle (Lonicera)

These material create a lime-green arrangement that would look spendid in a glass trough, half-framing a mirror.

Alternative Container

A silver trough would look striking with the white collection. Other types and colours of flowers could be arranged in troughs of metal, pottery and glass. Painted baking tins are useful; little of the container need be seen. A lidded basket or box such as a writing or needlework box is suitable with the appropriate choice of flowers.

Occasion

The arrangement would be ideal for a matching pair at the chancel steps in a church for a wedding. Arrange the highest points on the right in one arrangement and on the left in the other. Some churches also permit flowers on the altar, where these would also be suitable. The white flowers show up well, even if the church is poorly lit.

L-SHAPED LINE ARRANGEMENT

Plant Material

11 yellow carnations
5 yellow croton leaves from a pot plant
11 alder branches

Container

A cream rectangular ovenproof dish with a large, heavy pinholder

Creating the Arrangement

First place the pinholder to the side where the height will be in the arrangement, which way the L goes depending on its situation in the room. In this arrangement the pinholder is on the left, near the back of the container and a short way in from the side. When using branches in a line arrangement, it is best to establish the outline of branches first: the height, the widest points, and the longest over the front edge.

Often on branches there is a secondary branch a short way from the top; this can be used as the second or third longest branch, as has been done in this arrangement, where I use it as a second stem. Place this branch, with the secondary on its left, firmly into the pinholder towards the back. Place a third branch a little shorter than the second on the opposite side of the tallest stem from the second one. The stems should be quite close together. Go to the rim on the right side of the dish for the widest point; the longest side alder goes here and is placed horizontally three-quarters of the way back, choosing a branch for its natural curve. It should come over the edge of the dish. Next place the widest point on the opposite side; this branch is approximately half the length of the alder on the right side; again try to choose one which curves naturally to this particular side. The

longest one at the front edge goes in the same line as the tallest one at the back, but low against the rim. Place a few more pieces of alder throughout the arrangement, taking care to preserve the L.

Place the carnations, following the line of the main outline points of alder but cutting them all a little shorter in stem. (See the picture.) Begin with a small-flowered one at the top, making sure each is approximately a head shorter but slightly larger-flowered than the previous carnation. Place one to the left and another to the right of the top flower and work forward on the pinholder, placing flowers quite close together. Go to the right side. Again following the line of the alder, place a small carnation horizontally against the rim, a flower on either side of it going towards the centre of the container, each a little larger and lifting up slightly. Place a small carnation over the front edge as the longest one. At this stage put in the five croton leaves, the smaller ones at the back and over the front edge, the largest in the centre. The one on the front edge stands to the right of the longest alder, and the one at the back faces towards it. The rest zigzag through, turning to the side in the centre.

Position the remaining four carnations: Place a large one in the centre, and go from side to side with the rest. Maintaining the L shape, build up a little near the centre, and try to have the flowers at equal distances. Intersperse some alder with the carnations. If any of the pinholder is visible, cover it with the leaves or grasses of the carnations that have been removed from their stems, or with small pieces of alder, especially pieces with small cones. The water in the dish should cover the pinholder so that all the stems will be in water.

Alternative Plant Material

9 dark-red tulips
11 stems Hamamelis mollis flowers
5 Bergenia leaves in autumnal shades
The dark-red tulips pick up the colour of the centre of the Hamamelis mollis flower.

Alternative Container

A wooden tray. For other flowers of different colours, any shallow oblong dish or plate and wickerwork trays. If the containers are not deep enough to hold water, place the pinholder in a small container.

Occasion

A useful arrangement for the home as the branches would last a long while and only the flowers need to be replaced. The arrangement could be used to half-frame a picture, in which case select flowers with colours that complement the painting.

A BASKET WITH A HANDLE

Plant Material

15 stems berried skimmia
9 stems berried cotoneaster
9 stems berried leycesteria
5 stems heather (Erica)
3 stems fennel
3 Mahonia aquifolium leaves

Container

A basket with a handle with a baking tin lining; inside is a piece of florists' foam with 50-mm/2-inch mesh wire netting over it (see pages 9–10)

Creating the Arrangement

When arranging plant material in a basket with a handle, .you want to see some of the handle in the completed arrangement. Hence the leaves and berries should be kept lower in the centre, although a few pieces need to be against the handle to soften the line. If too many leaves obscure the berries, carefully

remove a few. You complete the arrangement as you do a basic facing arrangement, but slightly wider, taking into consideration the shape of the basket. The main outline stems are three-quarters of the way back in the container; the tallest three at the top are a skimmia set close to the right side of the handle, a stem of cotoneaster fractionally shorter on the opposite side of the handle to the skimmia, and on the right side of the first skimmia another skimmia slightly shorter than the cotoneaster. The widest points at the sides are on the right a cotoneaster, and on the left a skimmia, each being the same length over the edge of the basket. A skimmia is the longest one over the front edge and is on the opposite side of the handle to the tallest skimmia at the back.

The groupings consist of skimmia and erica, high in the right to low on the left; and the fennel and cotoneaster the opposite way. The leycesteria goes with this group but is kept more central. The three mahonia leaves are placed in the centre. Join the principal outline points with plant material, keeping to the correct groups and creating a broken line around the edge. Leave some of the basket visible at the front edge. Place foliage low in the container to cover the wire netting. Put in plant material at varying lengths, still leaving part of the handle visible. Check the stems are all below the water line.

Alternative Plant Material

5 orange montbretia
3 orange marigold
5 green tobacco plant (Nicotiana)
5 blue scabious
3 red roses
7 pink antirrhinum
3 mauve flag iris
5 yellow golden rod
3 cream stock
9 stems Senecio greyi foliage
11 stems escallonia
5 hosta leaves

A collection of mixed garden flowers. Often florists sell assorted bunches in the summer that would be ideal for this arrangement.

Alternative Containers

For the berried collection, a copper pan with a handle. For other plant material, handled baskets of wickerwork, china and glass would be suitable according to the type and colour of the flower.

Occasion

The autumnal arrangement of berries and leaves would be good for almost any home; it would last well in centrally heated houses. Place it on a cupboard, window sill, or in a similar position. A country cottage makes an ideal setting for it.

SLENDER ARRANGEMENT

Plant Material

13 stems dried grasses
7 stems pressed bracken
9 stems dried honesty (Lunaria)
3 stems preserved box (Buxus) cut into smaller pieces
3 lotus heads
(see pages 20–21 for methods of preserving)

Container

A stone-coloured cylinder with a picture on it in browns and greens. The arrangement's colour scheme matches the colours from the vase. A block of dry florists' foam is wedged into the container.

Creating the Arrangement

The arrangement is a basic facing one (as shown on page 24–25) but is more slender, in keeping with the shape of the cylinder. A fairly small head of grass is placed in the first, three-quarters of the way back in the container and in a central position. Since the container is slender the grass should be more than one-and-a-half times the height of the container. On the left of the grass but shorter-stemmed is a piece of box, on the right side a second grass, a little larger but shorter-stemmed. For the widest points, use a piece of bracken on the left and an honesty on the right, these going into the florists' foam horizontally and approximately a quarter of the length of the tallest grass, since you require a thinner arrangement. For the longest point over the front edge in the centre, place a stem of box.

The grouping is like that of all facing arrangements: the honesty and box are high on the left to low on the right, and the grasses and bracken move the opposite way. The three lotus heads at the centre create the focal point; place them next: a small one over the front edge to the left of the longest box, another smaller one towards the back of the arrangement, and the largest in the centre. Keeping to the grouping, place various plant material around the outline, decreasing the stems quickly to obtain an elegant shape. Radiate the stems and avoid their crossing each other. Connect the plant material groups through the centre, and also build the flowers and leaves from the longest at the front to the tallest at the back. Short pieces cover the dry florists' foam and the back of the arrangement.

Alternative Plant Material

Fresh plant material can be used in the cylinder, still taking the colours from the container. Use florists' foam with a small piece of netting over it.
5 stems alder (Alnus)
5 green zinnia
9 green tobacco plant (Nicotiana)
3 small green hydrangea
3 stems Berberis thunbergii Atropurpurea foliage
5 stems flowering cherry foliage

Alternative Container

A bamboo cylinder or tall thin urn in green or brown. Any slender urns, cylinders, or tall upright containers in various colours and made of various materials could have a similar arrangement with appropriate flowers and colour schemes.

Occasion

This is a winter arrangement used in the home or office. After use the plant material can be stored in a dry place for another year.